To A Beaut...

365 Days of Affirmations

for the Mind, Heart, Body, and Spirit

Thanks for being you

Written

&

Published

by

Phoenix Gibbs

Love Phoenix

Oracle/Healer, Ancestral Advocate, and Spiritual Mentor

Phoenix Gibbs specializes in mentoring and strengthening Spiritual Seekers in search of truth and a deeper understanding of who they are and how to serve humanity.

After almost losing her life in 2011, Phoenix Gibbs, a spiritual being having the most human of experiences, felt blessed with a second chance at life. Phoenix's near-death experience compelled her to dedicate this blessing to others and inspire them to live their lives right the first time around.

The theme of Phoenix's work is the realization that challenges are blessings in disguise which serve to teach us lessons as well as strengthen and prepare us for the beautiful manifestations we ask for in our lives.

Her mission is to encourage as many people as possible to live their best lives in real time without regret by stepping out of their comfort zones and trusting in themselves. Her goal is to remind others that even though they know their birth date and not their death date, they should not wait until something drastic happens to take charge of their lives.

This book of 365 affirmations was intentionally and authentically inspired by her challenges, her experiences, and all the lessons she has learned thus far. This book serves as a go-to guide for when anyone is in need of encouragement and inspiration right now in real time.

Phoenix sends love, light, compassion, kindness, integrity, respect, unity, authenticity, healing, health, abundance, gratitude, and prosperity to everyone reading this book.

Continue to be the change you would like to see in the world by showing up every day for yourself in the way you are serving, teaching, and sharing, because the world needs YOU!

She would like to thank her loving wife, Sabrina Gibbs, for her continuous love and support, as well as her family—friends included.

She would love to also thank God of her own understanding, as well as her angels, ancestors, grandparents, Mother Isis, and spiritual guides who love and protect her daily.

To everyone who has had the opportunity to read this book and who has been inspired in the most beautiful way, She pray that all your dreams become a reality and that you accept and embrace how amazing and powerful you are!

Day 1

I am blessed. I am worthy. I am valuable. I am loved. I am at peace. I am happy. I am confident.

Day 2

I honor my higher power who provides my needs, wants, and desires. I am filled with abundance, prosperity, health, and wealth, and I could not ask for anything better.

Day 3

I see pure love and beauty when I look in the mirror. I see a powerful masterpiece when I look in the mirror. I see my flaws and imperfections and I love everything about myself.

Day 4

I am my higher power's masterpiece. I was created with power and greatness within. There is no one like me. I am original. I am special. I am extraordinary.

Day 5

I continue to keep pushing regardless of the challenges I face. These challenges make me stronger, wiser, and more confident, and for that, I am thankful.

Day 6

I wholeheartedly honor myself by releasing what no longer serves me in order to make space for abundance and prosperity.

Day 7

My higher power created me in the most authentic and magical way. I accept all parts of myself without judgment. I treat myself with pure and unconditional love, compassion, kindness, and respect.

Day 8

I no longer give my power to others, as the only validation needed is my own. That in itself is enough.

Day 9

Self-love includes standing in my worth, my truth, my integrity, and my respect.

Day 10

I am here in this world to love, serve, teach, and share. I have no space for judgment, prejudice, discrimination, or hate.

Day 11

I consistently invest in myself so that I can truly grow into the person I know and feel myself becoming.

Day 12

I continue to show up and show out in my purpose regardless of how many times I fail or fall. Failure is not an option and I continue to rise up each time I fall down.

Day 13

I know my birth date, but I don't know my death date, so it is my responsibility to live my life to the absolute fullest and take action to do everything that makes my heart and spirit smile.

Day 14

I accept all my flaws and imperfections, as they are a part of me. I no longer beat myself up and I no longer have expectations of how life is supposed to be. I practice trusting and going with the flow.

Day 15

I embrace all the scars and imperfections on my body because they symbolize strength, courage, and love.

Day 16

I fearlessly use my voice to express how I feel. I free myself of silence when things feel unjust and unfair.

Day 17

I am creating amazing opportunities with my gifts, strengths, and talents because the world is waiting to see and experience what I have to offer.

Day 18

I am invincible, talented, strong, valuable, confident, special, and important! There is nothing I cannot achieve because I persist until the impossible happens.

Day 19

I give myself permission to spiritually see, feel, hear, and know spirit on a deeper level without fear and distrust.

Day 20

I was born to shine with all the greatness and power within me. I do not allow anyone or any circumstance to dim my light.

Day 21

I hold myself accountable and responsible for all the parts and roles I have played in my life, whether they were good, bad, or indifferent.

Day 22

I approach myself, as well as others, with unconditional love, compassion, kindness, honesty, and integrity because we are all imperfect spiritual beings having a human experience.

Day 23

I remain dedicated to self-love and self-care. I do not allow life and work to prevent me from taking care of my mental, emotional, and spiritual health.

Day 24

I cherish every aspect of who I am. I do not beat myself up for mistakes I have made and I release regrets that hold me back.

Day 25

I release the negative thoughts and stories I create when fear or challenges occur by reminding myself that they are false evidence and not who I truly am.

Day 26

I no longer allow fear to stop me from living my best life. I stretch and step outside of my comfort zone to experience the very best that life has to offer me.

Day 27

I give myself permission to release anxiety, depression, and anything else that no longer serves me so that I can truly step into my greatness, power, and purpose.

Day 28

I honor every feeling I experience, whether it be anger, rage, hurt, disappointment, betrayal, peace, happiness, joy, or fear. These are my feelings and I no longer choose to ignore them.

Day 29

I honor every "Aha" moment revealed and lesson learned. I apply these moments and lessons to my life so that I can continuously evolve and grow.

Day 30

I speak life over my circumstances daily. I replace negative words and thoughts with powerful, positive affirmations to help shift self-limiting beliefs.

Day 31

I am dedicated to healing internally so that I can finally release past trauma that no longer belongs in my heart and spirit.

Day 32

I accept every experience and challenge that prepares and strengthens me for the amazing blessings that are coming my way.

Day 33

I fearlessly and powerfully accept the spiritual evolution taking place in my life. I surrender to releasing the old me so that I can transform into the new me.

Day 34

I possess a powerful belief system about myself that is filled with faith, confidence, courage, honesty, transparency, and fearlessness.

Day 35

I exude confidence and courage, especially during difficult times, and I do not allow challenges to make me feel weak or bad about myself. I take charge of my thoughts and feelings, turning negative thoughts and feelings into positive ones for a powerful outcome.

Day 36

I am confident that all my needs are met. I trust my higher power to provide opportunities for my dreams to become my reality.

Day 37

I give my mind permission to replace negative thoughts with positive and powerful affirmations that help to change the way I feel about myself.

Day 38

My failures are still a part of my success because I am still giving it my all, regardless of the setbacks I may experience along the way.

Day 39

My imperfections make me perfect. I honor and embrace all my imperfections and I take pride in being my unique and beautiful self.

Day 40

I no longer beat myself up for things I have done wrong and I give myself credit for how far I have come on my journey.

Day 41

I acknowledge that my life is amazing regardless of challenges that may occur. I remain grateful instead of complaining about things that are not in my control because there is always someone else out there who is experiencing worse circumstances.

Day 42

I am grateful for the gift of life. I am grateful for the gift of my heartbeat. I am grateful for clarity. I am grateful for the opportunity to live this life.

Day 43

I choose to pray and manifest with trust, confidence, and peace of mind because the Universe always finds a way to take care of my every need, want, and desire.

Day 44

I remind myself daily that I am exactly where I am supposed to be and that I am being prepared for something powerful.

Day 45

I was built to be unstoppable, unbreakable, and unshakeable. There is nothing, big or small, that I can't handle or overcome.

Day 46

I show appreciation to those who have not given up on me and who choose to love me unconditionally despite all my flaws and imperfections.

Day 47

I honor and confront the pain from my past trauma so that I can finally heal my mind, heart, and spirit.

Day 48

I choose to take the necessary action to make all my dreams become reality. I do not allow anything or anyone, including myself, to stop me from being the very best I can be.

Day 49

I choose to work on myself daily, regardless of how discouraged I may feel due to things in my life not working out the way I desire them to.

Day 50

I give myself grace and compassion when things are not going my way. In these moments, I take a step back to see things from a higher perspective.

Day 51

I rest and replenish when I am tired. I do not push myself too hard when my body is telling me to recharge.

Day 52

I practice looking at myself in the mirror daily. When I look in the mirror, I fall in love with the amazing and powerful soul staring back at me.

Day 53

I remain dedicated to healing my heart and spirit because past trauma no longer has control over my life. I give myself permission and I have the willpower to release all the hurt and pain I feel in order to finally feel complete.

Day 54

I am grateful for everything I have in my life and everything that is to come.

Day 55

I am a walking manifestation of greatness.
This greatness touches everyone I encounter
each and every day.

Day 56

I say YES to all opportunities that feel right in my spirit instead of allowing fear to stop me from stepping into my blessings.

Day 57

I choose to welcome not only the wonderful, but also the uncomfortable, transformations I am experiencing. I see these transformations as blessings that will carry me to the upcoming chapters of my life.

Day 58

I am getting rid of any negative energy and toxicity I have created. I choose to remove myself from negative situations and individuals in order to protect my peace and sanity.

Day 59

I am an intentional being who wants the best for myself and others. It makes me happy to see other people win in life because it gives me inspiration. I am not envious of others.

Day 60

I strive to set honest and transparent examples for future generations. I exemplify integrity and a positive outlook on life, and I strive to inspire others to do the same.

Day 61

I work on my deep connection and relationship with my higher power daily so that I am able to truly show up and show out in the world.

Day 62

My beliefs and actions are powerfully limitless in all that I am and all that I do.

Day 63

I may not be able to control what takes place in my life. However, I can control my attitude and my feelings. I can choose how I want to move forward.

Day 64

I call on my higher self when I am feeling conflicted and confused about circumstances in my life. I put into perspective how precious and short life is, which brings me back full-circle to positive thinking and being.

Day 65

I take charge of self-limiting beliefs and replace them with self-limitless beliefs because I know and believe that my possibilities and opportunities are endless.

Day 66

I no longer feel guilty about having wants and desires because I deserve all the blessings life has to offer me.

Day 67

I no longer feel guilty about setting boundaries regarding what I will and will not tolerate from others.

Day 68

I honor my integrity and authenticity by no longer doing things that do not align with my heart and spirit.

Day 69

I honor myself by being clear in my communication with others and standing my ground about how I feel.

Day 70

I do not take things personally when it comes to rejection and disappointment because everything happens for a reason and for my greatest good.

Day 71

I embrace love, compassion, and kindness from others without guilt or shame because I deserve to receive as much as I give.

Day 72

I choose to laugh, love, and live as much as possible until I take my last breath.

Day 73

I choose to look at my past experiences as lessons, not mistakes or regrets. I am still here, living, overcoming, and surviving with confidence and strength.

Day 74

I own my vulnerability, as it is a strength and not a weakness.

Day 75

I am equipped with wisdom, talents, courage, and confidence to exceed my wildest dreams because I completely believe in myself.

Day 76

My positive and authentic presence makes an entrance before I do. I am unforgettable due to my pure heart and infectious spirit.

Day 77

I am no longer afraid to step into my greatness and power because they have been seeking me as much as I have been seeking them.

Day 78

Time waits for no one. I am not waiting to speak my truth, own who I am, and live my best life.

Day 79

I am not in competition with anyone. I embody all that was given to me on a unique vibrational frequency, which I claim and embrace.

Day 80

I forgive myself for any self-sabotaging thoughts and patterns I put myself through when I was hurt and in deep pain. I did not realize the harm I was causing myself.

Day 81

I no longer judge other human beings on how they react to situations in their personal lives because I don't know their stories and could not walk a day in their shoes.

Day 82

I choose to ask others, "How can I support you?" instead of thinking about what I can get from others. Situations do not always have to be about me because there are others who need a helping hand and a listening ear.

Day 83

I trust the process and have patience when I send out prayers to the Universe. I believe that things will take place in divine timing and divine order.

Day 84

I do my absolute best to release my worries and fears into the Universe by setting powerful intentions and vibrating higher in my beliefs.

Day 85

My days of seeking acceptance and validation from others are over. The only validation and acceptance needed are my own, which is more than enough.

Day 86

There is no need to have a sense of entitlement. No one owes me anything and I owe no one anything. I take full responsibility and accountability for my life.

Day 87

My days of depending on others to take care of my responsibilities are over. I choose to stand on my own and declare my independence.

Day 88

My days of overextending to feel accepted are over. My energy and time are valuable and I use them wisely. I no longer drain my energy and spirit by extending them to people who are not deserving.

Day 89

I will become everything that no one believed I could be. I believe in myself and I do the best I can with determination and dedication because my purpose is so much bigger than me.

Day 90

I express myself in the most authentic and transparent way possible, even if it makes others uncomfortable, because speaking my truth gives me ultimate freedom.

Day 91

I no longer allow anger to take away my joy and peace. I give myself permission to hold a five-second pity party and honor my anger. Then, I return to my peaceful center of being.

Day 92

I continue to do the right things even when my effort does not feel appreciated. I am doing this for myself and no one else. I honor self-appreciation because it creates positive karma in my life.

Day 93

My gifts are absolute blessings in my life and I share them proudly with the world. My gifts hold a higher purpose than I could ever imagine in this life. I honor and celebrate my gifts.

Day 94

I prefer to acknowledge others for their hard work and achievements rather than secretly hold jealousy and envy toward them because I will never know how much they sacrificed and suffered to get to where they are.

Day 95

My rock bottom has been an absolute blessing because it has made me extremely thankful for, grateful for, and strong in how far I have come in my life.

Day 96

I no longer use fear as an excuse for why I am not where I want to be in life. I choose to take action and do something about my current situation that will create a successful future.

Day 97

I am phenomenal. I am one of a kind. I am authentic. There is no one else like me in the world. I am exceptional. I am a leader. I am destined for greatness. I am special. I am important. I AM!!!

Day 98

I focus on what is going right in my life
instead of what is going wrong because my
thoughts become my reality.

Day 99

I know my birth date and not my death date. Until that time, I promise to live my life authentically and passionately, doing all the things I love.

Day 100

I speak up for myself, no matter how uncomfortable it may feel, because I refuse to suffer in silence. My voice is extremely important.

Day 101

Baby steps are just as important as adult steps when it comes to healing and transformation. I honor my baby steps and my adult steps, and I pat myself on the back for doing my best.

Day 102

I give myself credit for the things I have done right in my life and I celebrate every accomplishment, whether big or small, because they are all important.

Day 103

I trust my intuition, as it is a powerful blessing that helps me to make major life-changing decisions.

Day 104

I no longer feel bad about the things I have outgrown. I let them go in order to make space for the things that are truly important for my growth.

Day 105

I choose to stop complaining about things going wrong in my life. Instead, I practice gratitude for the things I have.

Day 106

I make change happen by shifting my mindset and perspective in order to create the life I truly desire and deserve.

Day 107

I am committed to inner healing, inner work, and introspection. These tools help me become the person I want to be by helping me let go of fear, guilt, and shame.

Day 108

I no longer feel ashamed about my spiritual beliefs because they are a part of who I am, regardless of how others may feel or think. I stand strong in the person I am becoming—a spiritual being having a human experience.

Day 109

I choose to break away from the conditioning I received during my upbringing. I am working toward establishing my own beliefs and creating the life I desire.

Day 110

I choose to live my full life's potential because I owe it to myself after all the struggles I have endured. I owe it to myself to truly stand in my power.

Day 111

I am capable of all the things I set my mind to doing in my life. I do not allow fear or doubt to prevent me from doing what I know in my heart needs to be done.

Day 112

I am no longer anyone's doormat or punching bag. I no longer accept any forms of negative or bad behavior from others that I don't even tolerate from myself. Those days are over.

Day 113

My healing is a process that will take time. I am determined to put in the work that results in permanent happiness and peace in my mind, heart, and spirit.

Day 114

I am determined to transform past trauma into triumph in order to powerfully experience the life that I desire and deserve.

Day 115

The Universe is so aligned with my energy and spirit that I am able to magically manifest my dreams and desires.

Day 116

Running from fear and confrontation no longer exists in my life. I face my fears with confidence and courage to ensure that my life is filled with fearlessness and unwavering faith.

Day 117

I feel and know that I deserve all the amazing opportunities the Universe is preparing on my behalf. I wholeheartedly accept these blessings with open arms.

Day 118

NO is a word I no longer fear and am not afraid to use. I do not feel guilty when I say **NO** to things that I don't believe in or care for.

Day 119

I am exactly where I am supposed to be. I am being prepared and strengthened for the evolution and journey that is about to take place.

Day 120

I say YES to myself and choose myself every time because I am worth it.

Day 121

My healing is ugly, painful, scary, and uncomfortable, but also beautiful, powerful, and very necessary for my growth.

Day 122

My honesty and transparency may make others uncomfortable; however, it is my responsibility to ensure that my truth is spoken and generational curses are broken.

Day 123

I honor my ancestors by being the best version of myself I can be. I use the integrity and strength that were created by their wisdom and courage, which run through my veins.

Day 124

I honor myself mentally, emotionally, physically, sexually, and spiritually, because this is what makes me feel complete and whole.

Day 125

My definition of success is being completely in tune with my higher self and being filled with happiness, peace, and wholeness.

Day 126

My hardships make me stronger. I go harder each day for the things that I desire.

Day 127

I do not complain about my circumstances because there are others who have it way worse than I do. I remain in a mindset of gratitude and continue to speak positivity over my life.

Day 128

Being selfish means making myself my top priority over everyone and everything instead of putting myself last.

Day 129

To me, it is very important that I use my voice and speak my truth. I express myself and allow my feelings to be heard without hesitation or explanation.

Day 130

My confidence allows me to use my voice as a powerful tool for self-expression, despite the opinions of others.

Day 131

I no longer fear being open and honest about my reality of turning my struggles into triumph. My story can help someone else.

Day 132

I see things for what they are and I see people for who they are. It is not my place to judge because I am just as flawed.

Day 133

Difficulty and disappointment are components of acceptance and growth that teach me valuable lessons.

Day 134

I accept what I cannot control and I release the need to know every single detail of any given outcome by trusting that it will turn out in my favor.

Day 135

I no longer enable myself with bad behavior and habits that leave me feeling depleted and discouraged. I take full responsibility and check with myself regarding things that are no longer working in my life. I make the proper changes for things to happen the way I desire them to.

Day 136

I offer myself tough love to help myself muster up strength in challenging times when I feel the need to give up.

Day 137

I practice self-honesty instead of remaining in denial about the cycles of dysfunction and discomfort I have put myself through. I take action toward improving my life patterns.

Day 138

I owe it to my ancestors to take my place as a leader by honoring them in the ways I show up each day of my life.

Day 139

My drive and determination do not allow me to give up on myself, especially when hardships are out of my control. I continue to strive and push until I experience my breakthrough.

Day 140

My lessons and mistakes teach me to appreciate everything in my life and every experience that is good, bad, and indifferent.

Day 141

Each morning, when I open my eyes and take my next breath, is an opportunity to express gratitude for everything I have in my life.

Day 142

I take the time to listen and feel my heartbeat, as it is one of the most amazing blessings I could ever ask for. I don't take my heart for granted and I make sure to keep it emotionally, physically, and spiritually fed.

Day 143

Limitations no longer stand in the way of my blessings. I am fully clear on my purpose and I have set intentions to make sure that my purpose is fulfilled in the most authentic and powerful way.

Day 144

I continue to build myself up and I do my best to keep a positive perspective on how great my life is, especially when things go wrong. I am my own motivator!

Day 145

I respect myself and honor my integrity by walking away from situations that no longer serve me. I am no longer willing to have my energy and spirit drained by toxic situations and people.

Day 146

I take back the power I gave to my past trauma because I am no longer the person who I was when I experienced the trauma. I stand tall and strong by owning my worth and walking in my triumph!

Day 147

I am amazing and powerful at speaking positivity over my life every single day. I am worthy and I deserve all the amazing things that the Universe is blessing me with every second of the day.

Day 148

I live in the now and I do not revert back to the past. The way I live my life now will create the future I desire and deserve. My future depends on every decision I make in the present. I choose happiness, peace, abundance, and prosperity.

Day 149

I no longer practice procrastination and I honor each step I take to make my life more enriching and enlightening. I do not wait for the "right" moment because I make each moment right.

Day 150

I release the need to be right and I relinquish the need to control everything taking place in my life. I trust the Universe to make things happen on my behalf in divine timing and divine order.

Day 151

I practice unconditional love and compassion with no judgment when it comes to self-love and self-forgiveness. I am imperfect and I will continue to make mistakes. I give myself grace and kindness for doing my best.

Day 152

The best gift I have given myself is permission to speak my truth and set myself free with no more excuses, explanations, or external validation.

Day 153

I love and honor every part of my body from my head to my toes. I appreciate and love myself, regardless of my scars and imperfections. I am deserving of self-love.

Day 154

I jump, stretch, and step outside my comfort zone to experience life at its finest. There is so much more that life has to offer me and I take advantage of every opportunity to create lasting memories by living my best life.

Day 155

I can, and will, have it all by doing the work and putting in the time. My sacrifices, frustrations, and failures are all part of the plan to keep me humble and appreciative of the greatness that is being created through my hard work.

Day 156

I feed and nurture my mind, body, heart, and spirit with positivity and goodness. I practice optimism as opposed to pessimism when obstacles and situations occur. I always remember that I deserve the best life has to offer me.

Day 157

I am a survivor of all that I have overcome thus far and what is yet to come. I speak my desires into the Universe in order for life to truly happen the way I desire it to.

Day 158

I don't owe anyone any explanations about how I choose to think, feel, behave, and live my life. I own my life and my destiny!

Day 159

Growth means learning lessons and applying them to my daily life on my journey to discover more about myself mentally, emotionally, physically, sexually, and spiritually.

Day 160

Conquering my fears means allowing myself to feel uncomfortable, nervous, anxious, and stressed. It means trusting the unknown and putting one foot in front of the other, moving forward no matter the outcome.

Day 161

I am forever growing and evolving during each year of my life. I welcome growth and I learn from each experience and situation that creates more wisdom. My growth will not stop until I take my last breath.

Day 162

I am mindful of the words I use when I am frustrated and angry because my words have power and the Universe is listening. I speak power and positivity over my life, especially when challenges unexpectedly occur.

Day 163

I reset my thoughts so that they align with my beliefs and feelings about myself. I no longer allow past trauma or judgment from others to cause me to revert back to negative thoughts and feelings. Positive thinking leads to positive results.

Day 164

My obligation to myself is to live my best life with honesty, integrity, unconditional love, and compassion.

Day 165

I declare my best life. I honor my best life. I claim my best life. I own my best life. I am experiencing my best life. I am living my best life.

Day 166

I am exactly where I need to be and I am exactly who I need to be at this moment while also welcoming and embracing where I am going and who I am becoming.

Day 167

I practice inner healing. I honor the parts that I have played in my life and I use each experience as a stepping stone to get to my next level.

Day 168

Every experience and challenge that I encounter on my journey teaches me strength, wisdom, and courage, and increases the love I have for myself.

Day 169

I no longer use the word "try" because I now take action in order to achieve the results I desire.

Day 170

I honor myself by creating my very own spiritual beliefs based on my feelings and experiences, which align with the life I am creating for myself.

Day 171

I choose consistency instead of contradiction by holding myself accountable for what I say, what I do, and how I live.

Day 172

I celebrate and gain inspiration from others instead of envying of their success. My time to experience success will come as long as I am patient, consistent, and doing my work.

Day 173

I forgive myself for putting myself through self-sabotaging situations because I was abused, hurt, and angry. I forgive myself for allowing past trauma to get the best of me. Forgiveness is ugly and uncomfortable, but also extremely necessary for true inner peace and happiness.

Day 174

I forgive myself for being selfish, hurtful, and manipulative toward others in order to get what I wanted. I forgive myself for using my past trauma as an excuse. I forgive myself for allowing fear to make me reject my very own power and greatness.

Day 175

I forgive myself for the levels of hurt and disrespect that others experienced because I did not know how to control my hurt and pain.

Day 176

I forgive myself for not asking for help when I needed it. I forgive myself for continuing to suffer in silence because I feared judgment and did not want to seem weak and vulnerable.

Day 177

I take back the power that I gave to my past trauma. I let go of the need to be a victim because doing so does not serve me.

Day 178

I take back my power from those who I gave permission to use me at my most vulnerable state.

Day 179

I ask for forgiveness from those who I used to get what I wanted when I was in a dark space, when I was not being genuine and intentional.

Day 180

I ask the little person within me for forgiveness because I put her in harm's way when she was seeking love and support instead of hurt from past trauma.

Day 181

Loving up on MYSELF. Appreciating MYSELF. Accepting MYSELF. Embracing MYSELF.

Day 182

I am proud of emotional, mental, physical, and spiritual evolution. I accept and embrace what is in store for by surrendering to my powerful evolution.

Day 183

Allowing the world to truly see me for everything I am: good and bad. That is the only way I know how to be. I am comfortable with and confident in my imperfections.

Day 184

Living in my legacy! Breathing and living—not just existing! Being thankful for every waking moment! Experiencing life at its finest no matter the obstacles! Being a blessing just because! This is how I was created!

Day 185

I release the chains of fear, doubt, anger, bitterness, and rage that I have been carrying. They no longer hold me back from being my best self and living my best life. The more I hold myself back and make excuses, the less I will get to experience life at its finest. I am not bound by those chains anymore!

Day 186

I am the starring role in my own feature presentation called life. I have one opportunity to make a lasting impression and legacy. The way I live my life and the positive affirmations I send into the Universe determine the Oscar and Emmy awards I will receive. I have what it takes to win!

Day 187

I do not feel the need to point fingers and blame others for my faults and actions. I remind myself that when I do this, there are three fingers pointed back at me.

Day 188

I am addicted to being uncomfortable and stepping outside of my comfort zone. Doing so causes me to experience things on deeper levels beyond my own understanding, and for that, I am grateful.

Day 189

I embrace every stretch mark, every scar, and every imperfection on my body. I practice body confidence. I no longer speak negativity over my body to suit the standards of society.

Day 190

I no longer wait until something drastic takes place in my life to take action. I make things happen in real time because time waits for no one and I refuse to have regrets on my deathbed. I am making moves right now!

Day 191

I am living life on purpose and living in my purpose because I was chosen. I choose to take my place in this beautiful life to serve, teach, and share.

Day 192

When I feel discouraged, I take a deep breath and listen to my heart for inspiration. That in itself is a powerful gift that can be taken away from me at any second.

Day 193

I honor my healing process right where I am.
I respect all the feelings I experience instead
of ignoring them. I confront all my emotions
and feelings and sit in them in order to truly
heal.

Day 194

I honor my intuition. My intuition guides me to where I need to go. It gives me clarity, as well as answers to the hard decisions I am conflicted and confused about making.

Day 195

I am victorious in my life's journey. I see things for what they are, control what I can, and leave the rest to my higher power. I no longer take on unnecessary stress from people or situations that do not concern me. I am focused on myself and what I need in order to gain peace and happiness within myself.

Day 196

I fearlessly and powerfully share my story with the world. Everything I have endured was designed to help others embrace their power and release their pain.

Day 197

I choose not to be defeated and I walk in confidence and faith, knowing that struggles and circumstances are temporary and my favorable outcome is permanent.

Day 198

I take full responsibility for everything that has taken place in my life because of the energy I chose to put out into the Universe, whether good or bad.

Day 199

I nurture the little person within me because that part of myself still needs to feel nurtured and protected in order for true healing to take place.

Day 200

I choose to have a fulfilled mind, heart, and spirit full of love, compassion, kindness, and peace instead of being bitter, angry, and hurt over things I cannot control or change.

Day 201

I love deeply and unconditionally. I am fortunate to feel and experience love at its finest because it is one of the most amazing gifts life has to offer.

Day 202

I don't want great, but I want extraordinary for my life! I am willing to work hard to achieve an extraordinary life with patience, perseverance, understanding, and dedication to myself!

Day 203

I may not have it all, but I am rich in health, happiness, and peace. I continuously claim positivity and expectancy of goodness over my life. I have no more excuses to make and I no longer procrastinate. I take action to obtain the things that I want for myself.

Day 204

I go with the ebbs and flows of life and I know that things are designed to take place for a reason. They are lessons meant to strengthen me with wisdom and experience.

Day 205

I can only do my best and honor my best efforts in my life. I release the need to control things that are not aligned with my passion and purpose.

Day 206

I acknowledge, appreciate, and give gratitude to every single moment of my life, from my heartbeat to my challenges and my accomplishments.

Day 207

My gifts and talents are gifts, not curses. I speak life over my gifts and talents. I accept them as part of who I am and what I am here to do in this world.

Day 208

I pay it forward and do the right things in my life with a giving and nurturing spirit because that is what we are supposed to do as human beings.

Day 209

I honor my higher power by showing up and showing out every single day, especially on the days when I don't feel like being my best.

Day 210

I honor my anger and pain. I ask myself how I can use these emotions to become a better human being who sees things from a different perspective.

Day 211

I remove thoughts and patterns of self-entitlement from my spirit and replace them with hard work, dedication, and selflessness.

Day 212

I am part of the human race and I choose to be loving and compassionate with no judgment, hatred, discrimination, or racism. We are all here going through struggles and fighting our way through our lives.

Day 213

No matter the obstacles and circumstances I may face, I choose to smile and give myself some compassion and grace.

Day 214

I refuse to allow fear to control my life. I take back my power and permission and I take leaps of faith to live my best life.

Day 215

I honor my weaknesses and strengths. I work on them daily, as I am a perfectly imperfect human being.

Day 216

I set realistic goals that honor my opportunities and possibilities in order to ensure my success in life.

Day 217

I give myself grace and forgive myself for past mistakes. I realize that it will take a process for me to experience true forgiveness and healing.

Day 218

I am constantly activating my greatness and power in every aspect of my life, as I owe it to myself to be the best that I possibly can.

Day 219

I inspire others by speaking my truth and sharing my story, struggles, and experiences, as so many people are suffering in silence.

Day 220

I appreciate waking up every morning and taking my next breath. I appreciate my five senses and the ability to experience the life that was given to me.

Day 221

I am grateful to have food in my fridge, clothes on my back, a bed to sleep in, and a home to live in. I am grateful for the small things and the big things taking place in my life.

Day 222

I am my greatest accomplishment and I honor myself by living my best life without regrets.

Day 223

I take positive risks right here, right now, in real time. I no longer doubt my self-worth, gifts, and talents.

Day 224

I take back my power from self-doubt, negative thinking, and fear. Fear doesn't live here anymore!

Day 225

I live in the present and no longer focus on the past. I am truly living, not just existing.

Day 226

I own and declare every second of my life because I can.

Day 227

I refuse to be average because I believe, feel, and know that I am extraordinary.

Day 228

I choose to RISE every time I fail or fall in my life. Feeling defeated will never be an option.

Day 229

My comeback is strong because I am driven, determined, resilient, and relentless.

Day 230

I will persist until the impossible happens!

My life is a phenomenal experience. It is done. So be it.

Day 231

I thrive regardless of my struggles because I CAN, I WILL, and I MUST.

Day 232

My life is a gift, a blessing, an experience, an accomplishment, and a beautiful manifestation.

Day 233

I excel at everything I set out to do for myself because being average is unacceptable.

Day 234

My new lifestyle is one of abundance and gratitude, and I am sticking to it!

Day 235

I am GREAT enough. I am STRONG enough. I am WORTHY enough.

Day 236

My inner healing leads to my long-term happiness. I put in the work and time to ensure that my ultimate goal in life—happiness and peace—is met.

Day 237

I trust my inner spiritual authority to lead me in the right direction and help me catapult forward in every aspect of my life.

Day 238

My life is a true spiritual gift that I do not take for granted.

Day 239

I am committed to self-growth instead of self-destruction.

Day 240

I wake up each morning with determination and passion because my dreams are waiting on me to make them my reality.

Day 241

I take action in real time, in my present, so that my future self will thank me for what I am creating here and now.

Day 242

Each rejection and disappointment only builds my character, strength, and determination to be greater today than I was yesterday.

Day 243

Going back to the drawing board is an exceptional blessing to start over and create another opportunity. I do not give up.

Day 244

Self-growth is an amazing gift that never stops giving. It offers wisdom, strength, determination, spiritual evolution, and freedom.

Day 245

I practice gratitude and appreciate all the abundance, prosperity, and excellence in my life instead of complaining about my struggles and circumstances.

Day 246

I practice self-compassion daily, especially when I don't feel like myself and when depression, anxiety, and fear start to set in. I do not allow my circumstances to steal my self-worth.

Day 247

I step into my greatness and power regardless of my struggles and past trauma. I free myself of mental, emotional, and spiritual prison.

Day 248

I refuse to allow hurt, pain, fear, and struggles to stop me from becoming an exceptional being who is ready for growth and change.

Day 249

I am thankful and grateful for my health, my home, my five senses, my beating heart, and my calm mind.

Day 250

I am dedicated to working hard because my next level is waiting on me.

Day 251

I replace excuses and explanations with action and accomplishments.

Day 252

I am a very important investment. This is
non-negotiable.

Day 253

HEALING

H means Health—how you create the life you are choosing to live.

E means Energy—what you put into the Universe and the attitude you display within yourself and toward others, which can be positive or negative.

A means Acceptance/Approval—your thoughts, words, and actions in how you choose to allow yourself, as well as others, to make you feel about your life.

Day 254

L means Love—the source of your emotions, whether you choose to be peaceful and happy or miserable and broken, not ready to heal.

I means Intuition—the source of the decisions, avoidance, mistakes, and regrets you will experience, whether they be good and bad. Always remember that it is never too late for new beginnings.

N means New—starting over, beginnings, opportunities, potential, leaps of faith, capabilities, and newfound confidence within yourself.

Day 255

G means Gratitude—why you wake up in the morning with purpose and ambition; why you want to achieve more tomorrow than you did today. Practicing gratitude is doing your best to take yourself to the next level because you know life is too short and time is of the essence.

Day 256

I am creating my very own definition of success that consists of my experiences, struggles, lessons, and honesty about who I am and what I want.

Day 257

Giving up on my dreams because things are not going as expected is not an option. There will always be obstacles along the way, but giving up is never an option.

Day 258

I am creating the life I want without excuses, explanations, or apologies. I no longer hold myself back and I will make change happen. My healing is based on the growth I gain from doing my work and putting in the necessary time.

Day 259

I take ownership of and responsibility for my voice. I speak and live my truth in order to set myself free.

Day 260

I release the chains of fear, doubt, anger, bitterness, and rage I have been carrying. They no longer hold me back from living my best life.

Day 261

I give myself permission to explore and experience life at its finest with no excuses or explanations. I honor my heart's desires and make all my dreams my reality.

Day 262

I no longer run from hardships. Instead, I confront them with confidence, courage, and compassion. I allow my hardships to strengthen me so that I can do great things in my life. I see hardships as gifts for greatness instead of curses for struggle.

Day 263

I shift my thoughts and energy to align with the Universe in order to manifest my life's desires and dreams. It all begins with me.

Day 264

My healing begins with freedom of expression. I express how I truly feel about past trauma, struggles, hurt, and pain in order to truly set myself free.

Day 265

I ask myself for true forgiveness daily. I apologize to myself for beating myself up for past mistakes and for holding myself hostage to pain and sadness instead of releasing what no longer serves me.

Day 266

I no longer enable any forms of self-destructive behavior. I confront my negative behaviors and self-sabotaging ways with honesty, integrity, unconditional love, compassion, and no judgment.

Day 267

I release the spirits of hate, judgment, criticism, gossip, and envy from my mind and heart because I don't know others' struggles and sacrifices.

Day 268

I take control of my experiences and situations as they come and I do my best to live in each moment. I do my best to remind myself that life is precious and, indeed, very short. I attempt to make lasting and meaningful memories.

Day 269

I take care of myself and I nurture my spirit and heart by affirming myself each day that I am valuable and authentic. I remind myself that I deserve all that life is offering me.

Day 270

I allow my aura to shine so bright that it lights up every room I walk into. My purpose is so consistent that it causes a strong impact that others can feel within their minds, hearts, and spirits. My leadership is so strong and confident that it causes others to do better for themselves.

Day 271

Mistakes and regrets don't stop me from striving to do my best every day. These lessons and blessings push me to create better opportunities and possibilities for myself.

Day 272

Patience is required for me to honor true healing within myself. Patience is required on my journey to true self-discovery and self-acceptance. Patience is required for me to honor and accept true self-forgiveness.

Day 273

Everything in my life happens in divine order and divine timing. My responsibility is to go with the ebbs and flows of what takes place, seeing the blessing in each experience with gratitude.

Day 274

I refuse to feel, speak, and live an ordinary life, as being extraordinary is embedded in my DNA. I refuse to allow what I have been through to take away my dedication, determination, drive, and confidence to step into my greatness and power.

Day 275

My next level is waiting for me and I will not disappoint myself in getting there. I consistently do the necessary work and make sacrifices to get to where I need to be.

Day 276

My dreams and aspirations are not going to create themselves. I am so intentional that my dreams and aspirations are manifested in the most powerful way.

Day 277

Don't allow life to pass you by as you wallow in wanting everything to be perfect now. If you do, you will miss out on amazing revelations and "Aha" moments that help to build up your wisdom, strength, courage, and understanding.

Day 278

I am unbreakable! I am unshakable! I am unstoppable! This is my superpower!

Day 279

I am my greatest accomplishment. I have become so different than the person I used to be and I embrace the person I am becoming.

Day 280

I am loved. I am courageous. I am confident. I am wise. I am compassionate. I am kind. I am respectful. I hold integrity. I am determined. I am abundant. I am prosperous. I am grateful. I am all these things and more.

Day 281

I turn my trials and tribulations into triumph because I owe it to myself to live the life I deserve and desire.

Day 282

I own and celebrate every second of my life because I can and I truly deserve to.

Day 283

I refuse to be average because I am extraordinary, and I will not have it any other way.

Day 284

I choose to RISE every time I fail and fall. I always get back up because I declare my place in this world. I will never let myself down.

Day 285

I am determined! I am driven! I am resilient! I am relentless!

Day 286

My responsibility is to persist until the seemingly impossible happens—my dreams become my reality.

Day 287

My life is a phenomenal experience and I will not have it any other way, despite the past trauma and struggles I have experienced.

Day 288

My obligation to myself is to thrive regardless of my circumstances.

Day 289

I no longer take myself for granted. Now, I cherish every aspect of who I am and what I mean to myself.

Day 290

I CAN. I WILL. I MUST. There is no other way.

Day 291

I exceed all that I set out to do in all aspects of my life. I have an obligation to myself to want more and desire more.

Day 292

I stand on the shoulders of my ancestors because they have created a path for me to exceed and succeed in this life. I could not have done it without them.

Day 293

My happiness and success are happening right now, in real time.

Day 294

My lifestyle is one of abundance and gratitude. I wear this lifestyle daily with pride, courage, and confidence.

Day 295

I am valuable enough. I am confident enough.
I am courageous enough.

Day 296

I honor my hard work, struggle, and pain. My experiences serve to help me gain strength, wisdom, and courage.

Day 297

My inner healing leads to my long-term happiness and peace.

Day 298

I am committed to trusting my inner spiritual authority.

Day 299

My life is a spiritual gift that I cherish and appreciate, as it can be taken away from me at any given time.

Day 300

I am committed to my self-growth instead of my self-destruction.

Day 301

I make my dreams become my reality in real time.

Day 302

I always battle the storm before the calm comes, and I come out of this battle emotionally, psychologically, and spiritually stronger than I was before.

Day 303

I am responsible for what I think, how I act, what I say, and how I react to things in my life.

Day 304

I am living my life right the first time regardless of my obstacles.

Day 305

I am committed to living, not just existing, because I owe myself so much more.

Day 306

I was destined for greatness from the time I came out of my mother's womb. I am a trendsetter and a trailblazer in my very own extraordinary way. I own it. I declare it. I embrace it.

Day 307

I continue to effortlessly affirm greatness over my life and hold myself accountable for creating more greatness in my life.

Day 308

I created my own table instead of asking to sit at a table with people who do not acknowledge or appreciate what I have to offer.

Day 309

I am thankful for another day and another year in my life! I welcome the shifts and "Aha" moments that are given to me daily! I wake up knowing that great things and great people are coming my way! I wake up knowing that I deserve the best out of life. I speak my best into existence!

Day 310

I am passionate! When I do something, I am invested! I love hard, work hard, and play hard!

Day 311

My failures are not forms of defeat. Instead, they are lessons meant to help me navigate through life circumstances with deeper awareness and perspective.

Day 312

Lessons, growth, and healing will not stop until I take my last breath.

Day 313

I am exactly where I need to be in my life, in real time, at this very moment. I create my future by living intentionally in my present.

Day 314

I am destined for greatness. I am here to do great things. I was born to do great things. I am successful!

Day 315

Persistence, love, compassion, courage, wisdom, strength, consistency, integrity, dedication, and commitment are part of my DNA.

Day 316

I am committed to praying with faith, confidence, and conviction instead of with fear and doubt.

Day 317

My heart is filled with gratitude, abundance, and prosperity. I consistently speak greatness over my life and allow all my blessings to effortlessly flow through me.

Day 318

I say goodbye to regret, past mistakes, and trauma in order to step into my present moment with every fiber of my being. This will help to create a future filled with never-ending abundance and greatness.

Day 319

I live because it is what I choose to do. I laugh because I feel it in my soul. I love because my heart yearns for it and deserves it. I pray because it helps me to live, laugh, and love.

Day 320

I always want to improve my life and create more for myself. My possibilities and opportunities are endless and limitless.

Day 321

I am blessed and fortunate to wake up each morning. I am grateful for my health, shelter, clothes, food, transportation, and all the blessings I am experiencing right here, right now, in real time.

Day 322

I view my struggles and circumstances as lessons meant to strengthen me. These lessons prepare me to receive what I am asking for with gratitude and appreciation.

Day 323

My inner healing leads to my long-term happiness, as I am doing the work to get to where I want to be in my life.

Day 324

My prayers become reality when I am prepared to receive them and not take them for granted.

Day 325

I am a very important investment that is non-negotiable and I refuse to give up on myself.

Day 326

I no longer give my fears permission to control my life. I am willing to step outside of my comfort zone and take risks to live the life I truly desire and deserve.

Day 327

I am confident that my needs, wants, and desires are provided for in real time and that amazing opportunities are coming my way.

Day 328

I am breaking barriers, breaking rules, and being an authentic rebel in my life. My actions are not based on the life society has chosen for me. I choose to live out loud.

Day 329

I spiritually nourish my mind, heart, and spirit to create positive thinking, speaking, and living.

Day 330

My struggles are temporary and my gratitude is permanent because I know, feel, and believe that greater things are coming my way.

Day 331

The inner healing I experience may be ugly, messy, and uncomfortable, but it is extremely necessary for true healing to take place in all aspects of my life.

Day 332

I honor and accept every emotion I feel. I no longer resist or ignore my emotions because they are valid and ready to be freed.

Day 333

My past can no longer hurt me or haunt me unless I give it power to. My mistakes have no power unless I give them permission to hold power over me. Fear cannot control me unless I allow it to consume me. I choose to take my power and permission back.

Day 334

Part of my healing process is acknowledging the things I don't like about myself and making the necessary changes to turn those dislikes into loves.

Day 335

I was born worthy and I deserve all the blessings coming my way despite my past trauma. I honor my inner greatness and I release pain and tribulations.

Day 336

I continue to show up and show out in my life as I secretly inspire others who are watching.

Day 337

I no longer act with resistance because it blocks me from discovering who I truly am and from experiencing my best life. I choose to become limitless in my thoughts, words, and actions in order to create the circumstances I want.

Day 338

My setback was a powerful blessing for my comeback!

Day 339

I continue to speak my truth regardless of how uncomfortable it makes others feel. I have a responsibility to myself to be free from fear, guilt, and shame, and that comes with speaking my truth.

Day 340

I am kind and compassionate toward myself without expectations of instant gratification, especially when it comes to my inner healing.

Day 341

I continue to speak love over my life,
especially on days when I am feeling
unworthy and discouraged.

Day 342

I keep going regardless of the inner demons that try to shake me and break me. I am unbreakable and unshakable, with nothing stopping me from being my own light.

Day 343

I apologize to myself and forgive myself for putting myself last. I put myself first in the most loving and compassionate way.

Day 344

I am exactly where I need to be right now in my life. I relinquish the need to control every step because my path will be revealed to me sooner than I think in divine timing and divine order.

Day 345

I no longer abuse and punish myself for past trauma I did not cause. It was not my fault and I am much more valuable than my past trauma.

Day 346

I forgive myself because I have done nothing wrong. I am doing the best that I can.

Day 347

I am brave. I step out of my comfort zone in order to be seen and heard because my gifts cannot share themselves.

Day 348

I wake up every morning with determination and passion because my dreams are waiting for me to make them my reality.

Day 349

I pat myself on the back and give myself credit for not allowing past trauma to define who I am. I am a powerful and beautiful soul who deserves all the blessings coming my way.

Day 350

I constantly release what no longer serves me and I make room for the blessings that are waiting for me to receive them with open arms.

Day 351

I am dedicated to vibrating higher and showing gratitude for each blessing I receive. I am grateful for the blessings that are on their way to me right now in real time.

Day 352

My possibilities and opportunities are in my reach and nothing will stop me from receiving what is destined for me. I claim and declare what I desire and deserve.

Day 353

I am committed to self-care as a part of my healthy lifestyle because I matter. I treat myself in the most selfish, yet also authentic, way possible.

Day 354

I have overcome challenges. I have faced my fears. I have honored my inner knowing. I have stood in my convictions. I have spoken my truth. I have set myself free. I am living my best life.

Day 355

Nothing or no one can stop what is destined for me but me, and I choose to honor myself by exceeding all that I have set out to do for myself and my life.

Day 356

My healing truly begins by going through the inner pain. I allow myself to feel and confront the most hurtful parts of my life with confidence, courage, strength, self-love, and integrity.

Day 357

I teach what I have experienced and overcome in my life, as I am the expert of my life and it is my responsibility to serve, teach, and share.

Day 358

Today is my rebirth. I wake up and start over with pride, stepping into my greatness and embracing what life has in store for me.

Day 359

I walk in full abundance and prosperity
with courage, confidence, fearlessness and
unwavering faith.

Day 360

I am grateful for the power of choice. I am grateful for the gift of FREE will. I am grateful for life lessons.

Day 361

I have a high vibration. I am powerful in my frequency. I am an authentic light. I am one with the Universe.

Day 362

I evoke pure love. I evoke pure compassion. I evoke pure authenticity. I evoke pure peace.

Day 363

I am proud of my growth. I am proud of my breakthrough. I am proud of who I am.

Day 364

I am excited about my possibilities. I am excited about my opportunities. I am excited in advance for what's already mine.

Day 365

I surrender to my healing. I surrender to pure joy and peace.

I surrender to abundance and prosperity.

Connect with Oracle Phoenix Gibbs for intuitive oracle card readings, wisdom and insight sessions, and spiritual self-care bath products.